Taking Center Stage

Taking Center Stage
Drama in America

Teacher's Manual

Amy K. Rathburn

Ann Arbor

THE UNIVERSITY OF MICHIGAN PRESS

Copyright © by the University of Michigan 1997
All rights reserved
ISBN 0-472-08431-3
Library of Congress Catalog Card No. 96-61726
Published in the United States of America by
The University of Michigan Press
Manufactured in the United States of America

2000   1999   1998   1997   4   3   2   1

Acknowledgments

Grateful acknowledgment is made to the following publishers, newspapers, magazines, and authors for permission to reprint copyright material.

Fodor's Travel Publication for material from *Fodor's 96: Pocket New York City*. Copyright © 1996 by Fodor's Travel Publications, Inc. Reprinted by permission of the publisher.

Meriwether Publishing Ltd. for material from *TV Scenes for Actors* by Sigmund Stoler. Colorado Springs: 1989.

Random House, Inc. for material from *A Raisin in the Sun* by Lorraine Hansberry. Copyright © 1959, 1966, 1984 by Robert Nemiroff. Reprinted by permission of Random House, Inc.

The Condé Nast Publications, Inc., for material from *The Shadow*.

Capitol Records for the song recordings "Oh, What a Beautiful Mornin'" and "Oklahoma." Under license from EMI–Capitol Music Special Markets.

Contents

About This Book

Thank you for choosing *Taking Center Stage: Drama in America*. This text provides a general introduction to the history of drama in the English language and an overview of some of the popular theatrical, radio, television, and movie dramas currently presented in America. This text will provide students with a deeper understanding of popular American culture and literature and will also provide them with an opportunity to create and act in English in original dramatic scenes.

The text is designed for high-intermediate to advanced ESL students and has been taught successfully at these levels. Throughout the text students are encouraged to read, analyze, and act out scenes from a variety of authentic dramatic material (for example, Arthur Miller's *Death of a Salesman*). Though students may be a little hesitant at first, other teachers and I have found that the medium of drama has an almost magical way of "opening up" even the shyest student and of creating an atmosphere highly conducive to language use and improvement.

Chapter 1 introduces essential terminology and concepts of both drama and acting. Chapter 2 looks at the historical origins of drama in the English language and asks students to interpret scenes from several of the major historical periods. I recommend covering these chapters in detail because they provide the foundation for future chapters. The remaining chapters cover particular types of popular American drama, including Broadway musicals, sociorealistic plays, radio and television dramas, and American movies. In each of these chapters, students are provided with many opportunities to read, interpret, and act in authentic dramas and to create and act in original scenes.

Once you have covered chapters 1 and 2 it is not absolutely necessary to cover the remaining chapters in order. They are, however, arranged in a logical order both from a content standpoint and a language standpoint, and some of the activities may rely on knowledge of information from previous chapters.

As a teacher you do not need to have any knowledge of drama to teach this text; it has been successfully piloted with teachers who have little or no experience with the topic. One novice had this to say:

> "My students enjoyed learning cultural information about current and historical American dramatic entertainment, while I remained confident that they were developing and practicing useful and important language skills in the process. The drama writing and acting activities in each chapter lower students' inhibitions and allow them ample opportunity to utilize their creativity. A thoroughly enjoyable course to teach!"
>
> Kristen Sanford
> Michigan State University

I would welcome any suggestions you have for improving this text. Any comments can be sent to Amy Rathburn at Michigan State University, Room One, International Center, East Lansing, MI 48824-1035.

How to Use the Teacher's Manual

The teacher's manuals for the **Alliance** series were designed with two principal goals in mind: (1) to provide as much detail as possible for those teachers who are new to content-based language teaching (please use as much or as little of the information provided as you feel necessary); and (2) to develop an easy-to-follow format that is consistent throughout the text. This format follows that of the student's book and can be summarized as follows:

Opening Activity: This section describes the opening activity and its purpose.

Objectives for Students: This section parallels the "To the Student" section of the student's book but outlines *both* the content and language objectives for the chapter. You have the option of sharing the language objectives with the students.

Content Headings: The content headings follow exactly as they do in the student's book. Within each content heading, there are generally three sections:

> *Techniques:* For the relevant activities, the author will discuss the techniques, or approach, he/she has used to present the material to students. This discussion will be based on the author's actual experience and may or may not be used as a guideline for conducting the activity in class.

Answers and student handouts: Answers will be provided, as well as student handouts when appropriate. Answers will not be provided in cases where they may vary.

Scripts: All scripts from audiotapes (or videotapes) are provided.

Additional/Follow-up Activities: Suggestions for follow-up, supplementary, or alternative activities are provided when applicable.

I hope you find enough information here to feel confident in teaching the subject matter while feeling free to follow your personal teaching style. Suggestions are welcome and may be directed to Amy K. Rathburn at Michigan State University, Room One, International Center, East Lansing, MI 48824-1035.

Chapter 1

Introduction to Drama

Opening Activity

Tell students that four of the words in each set belong together, but one word does not. Ask students to find the one word in each set that does not belong. Then discuss the connections between each set of words (answers given are possible answers—students may find additional connections).

Answers

1. music; forms of drama
2. audience; jobs related to theater/drama
3. love; elements in (traditional) dramatic structure
4. history; related to a live dramatic production/things that create mood
5. gesture; vocal items/things connected to speech/acting

Objectives for Students

Content

Understand various dramatic forms and dramatic structure
Act out a scene from a famous American drama
Analyze a text for character development and setting
Analyze a text for use of movement and music
Write and act out a short drama

Language

Reading/Writing

Using the dictionary
Understanding organization of main ideas
Making outlines of a text
Note-taking skills and abbreviations
Inferencing
Writing a short drama
Finding definitions in a text

Speaking/Listening

Brainstorming
Taking lecture notes
Listening for details
Listening for main ideas
Speaking with appropriate stress and tone
Identifying mood and tone
Acting out a short drama
Recognizing nonverbal gestures

Chapter Activities

I. What Is Drama?

Techniques

The purpose of this section is to familiarize students with key terms, which
will be used throughout the book. Activity A is a matching exercise in which
students recognize and interpret various dictionary definitions and terms.
For Activity B, remind students that different dictionaries present information in different ways. Encourage students to create original answers for
Activity C.

Answers

A.   a. tragedy   b. actor   c. setting   d. plot

B. Etymology = 1, Part of speech = 6, Syllabification and pronunciation = 3, Cross-reference = 2, Meaning(s) of the word = 5, Inflected form = 8, Undefined form = 4, Abbreviation = 7

C. Answers will vary.

II. Dramatic Form

Techniques

In Activity A, students brainstorm a list of 10 dramas. These dramas might be plays, television shows, movies, and so on. If students have trouble, ask them to list their *favorite* dramas. They are asked to categorize their lists in Activity B. It is expected that dramas will not fall neatly into one category. Activity C explains various forms of drama. Activities D and E work with some of the vocabulary in the text by teaching students definition clues. For Activity F, students should review only the section on tragedy. Encourage students to use their own words, symbols, and abbreviations, and *not* to copy down sentences from the text. Activity G tests comprehension of the reading and note-taking abilities. Activity H can be given as homework. Remind students to use the categories comedy, tragedy, melodrama, and history. For Activity I, students are introduced to note-taking symbols and abbreviations. Activity K gives students a chance to share their own systems for writing symbols and abbreviations.

Answers

A./B. Answers will vary.

D. exact; the word *or*

E. 1. d; direct   2. e; direct   3. c; indirect   4. b; direct   5. a; direct

F.
I. *Tragedy*
    A. Explores serious questions, e.g.
        1. causes of evil
        2. value of pain & suffering
        3. meaning of life and death

B. Basic plot (story line) = simple
  1. hero (protagonist) good
    a. intelligence
    b. strength
    c. beauty
  2. hero becomes miserable
  3. sad ending; hero suffers & dies
C. Reaffirms dignity of humankind
D. e.g. = *Romeo and Juliet*

G.
II. *Comedy*
  A. Cmd. differs from trgd. in 5 ways
    1. chrctrs like ourselves, e.g.,
      a. make mistakes
    2. plot is as * as main chrctrs.
    3. happy ending, e.g.,
      a. people fall in love
      b. reunited
      c. get married
    4. mind   emotions
    5. reduces human dignity to laughable limitations
  B. e.g. = *The Simpsons*
III. *Melodrama*
  A. *popular in 19th & 20th C.
  B. (like trgd.) appeals to emotions
  C. suspenseful and fun
  D. often criticized
    1. plot = unbelievable
    2. chrctrs. = *good/*evil, e.g.,
      a. Batman
      b. Joker
    3. ending always happy (unrealistic)
  E. e.g. = Westerns, war movies, cops & robbers
IV. *Historical*
  A. realistic portrayal of people, places, times
  B. may contain fiction evnts./chrctrs.
  C. e.g. = Gandhi

I.

Symbols

1. equal (to)   2. and   3. important 4. greater than 5. or

Abbreviations

1. (for) example 2. comedy 3. tragedy   4. events   5. characters

J.

∧	∨
>	<
w/	w/o
′	″
∴	→
*	÷
%	&
≃	pp.
p.	@

K. 1. There is too little information to determine the meaning.
2. This abbreviation is all vowels and impossible to interpret.
3. There is too little information to determine the meaning.
4. This is probably a one-syllable word or there is too little information to determine the meaning.
5. This abbreviation won't save the writer any time because it is almost the same as the original word that's being abbreviated.

L. Possible answers include: 1. drm 2. prtgnst 3. mldrm 4. sttg
5. dgnty 6. cnclsn 7. strctr 8. cnflct 9. actn 10. rsltn

Additional Activity

Students form teams and choose one person to be the team "artist." The artist stands at the board and draws signs and abbreviations, which have been prepared by the teacher. The artist cannot talk or use gestures. Each team scores one point for every sign or abbreviation that they correctly guess. The team with the most points "wins."

M. Common abbreviations (meanings) include the following: A.D. (anno Domini), amt (amount), asst (assistant), avg (average), bet (between), bldg (building), Bsc (bachelor of science), chrn (chronological), cl (class), c/o (in care of), dbl (double), dir (director), edu (education), esp (especially), exp (expense), fem (female), genl (in general), hr (hour), hwy (highway), id (the same), intl (international), lit (literally), max (maximum), mid (middle), mo (month), natl (national), neg (negative), ofc (office), org (organization), pkg (package), prev (previously), QED (which was to be demonstrated), qty (quantity), req (required), RSVP (please reply), rte (route), sch (school), sm (small), std (standard), syn (synonymous), tot (total), usu (usually), VIP (very important person), vv (vice versa), yd (yard), yr (year), z (zero). Common symbols include the following: # (number of), $ (money), " " (quotes).

III. Dramatic Structure

Techniques

The purposes of this section are to practice note-taking skills and also to become familiar with traditional dramatic structure. In Activity A students should understand that not *every* idea (conflict) is appropriate for drama. Answers will vary, but make sure students justify their answers. Activity B is a listening/matching activity that introduces students to the meaning (and spelling) of basic structure terms. Play the lecture one or two times. You may also want to point out that not *every* drama has a clear-cut, five step structure and that some may seem to have no structure at all. For Activity C, play the script again as students take notes. For Activity D, students use their own notes to answer the questions.

Answers

A. 1. Possible commonalities include the following: conflict, mystery, love, pain and suffering.

Script

Structure of Drama

The structure of a traditional drama is created through a series of related events. This structure typically has *five steps,* which go up to a turning point and then go down. These five steps unfold the conflict and resolution between two of the main characters: the *protagonist,* or hero, and the *antagonist,* or villain. The conflicts that occur between the protagonist and antagonist can be physical. However, the conflict can also involve mental, spiritual, or philosophical differences. Here, then, are the steps of a traditional drama.

1. *Exposition and Initial Incident*

    In the opening scenes, we have the exposition and the initial incident. The exposition gives the audience key information about the drama, like the setting, the main characters, and the general situation and conflict. The mood and atmosphere are also set in the exposition, often through the costumes, lighting, props, and scenery.

The initial incident occurs within the exposition. This is the first important event to take place on stage and the point from which the rest of the plot develops. Consequently, the initial incident is very important; it must capture the attention of the audience and make the audience want to know what will happen next.

2. *The Rising Action*

The rising action is the series of events following the initial incident. These events serve to heighten the level of interest and suspense. During this early part of the play, the playwright may also choose to add other minor characters or interesting complications, which then develop into less important conflicts, or "subplots."

3. *The Climax*

The climax is the turning point of the play. It is the moment that determines what the final outcome of the main conflict will be. This is often a very thrilling moment, for example, a fight, murder, or wedding.

4. *The Falling Action*

The falling action is the series of events following the climax. It is usually shorter than the rising action, but the events must be of real significance and interest in order to hold the attention of the audience. Subplots are often brought to conclusion during the falling action, and minor characters somehow resolve their conflicts.

5. *The Conclusion and Denouement*

The conclusion of the drama is the logical outcome of all that has come before it. The success or failure, happiness or sorrow, of the characters must be the result of their own actions and/or nature. In most traditional dramatic structure (unlike melodrama) the conclusion is never the result of a previously hidden outside force, chance, or matter of luck.

One exception to this, however, is when a denouement is used. Denouements, which are often used in mystery dramas and soap operas, are surprising incidents or ingenious explanations that solve the secrets and puzzles connected with the conflict.

B. 1. e 2. a 3. d 4. c 5. g 6. b 7. f

C. *Possible Completed Outline*

Structure of Drama

I. Structure = series of rel. events
   A. 5 steps ∧ ∨
   B. unfold conflict between protagonist (hero) and antagonist (villain)
   C. conflicts may be
       1. physcl
       2. mntl
       3. sprtul
       4. philophcl
II. 5 Steps
   A. Exposition and Initial Incident
       1. Exposition
           a. Gives * info.
               i. setting
               ii. main characters
               iii. gnrl. situation & cnflt.
       2. Initial Incident
           a. 1st * event
               i. starts action
               ii. must hold attention
   B. Rising Action
       1. events after init. inc.
       2. all add interest/ suspense
       3. + of minor chars.
       4. + subplots (less important conflicts)
   C. Climax
       1. turning pt.
       2. determines outcome
       3. *thrilling, e.g.,
           a. fight
           b. murder
           c. wedding

    D. Falling Action
        1. events after climax
        2. shorter than rising action, but *
            a. subplots resolve
            b. minor chars. resolve cnflcts.
    E. Conclusion and/or Denouement
        1. Conc.
            a. logical outcome
            b. result of actions or nature
        2. Denouement
            a. Mystery drama and soap opera
            b. surprise incident/ingenious explanation
                i. solve conflict

D.

1. Conflict often occurs between the antagonist and protagonist. Examples include mental, spiritual, philosophical, or physical conflict.
2. A. exposition B. initial incident C. rising action D. climax E. falling action F. conclusion
3. A denouement comes in the conclusion and provides a clever or surprising explanation or solution.
4. a subplot
5. In traditional drama, no. In melodrama or soap operas, sometimes.

IV. Character and Setting

Techniques

In this section students are asked to read (or act out) a scene from Arthur Miller's *Death of a Salesman* and to infer information about character and setting. Depending on the level of your students, you may wish to do some vocabulary work with the passage. For Activity A, arrange pairs and en-courage students to read as if they were acting and to follow italicized stage directions (it may help to ask students to stand up when acting out the text). Students may be shy about acting and need a lot of encouragement! For Activities B, C, and D, a few answers are stated directly in the text, but most need to be inferred. Consequently, possible answers are given here. Remind students that there is not one correct answer. It is, however, impor-tant that answers be logical and supported by the text.

Answers

B. 1. b 2. b 3. c 4. c 5. a

C. 1. a 2. c 3. b

D. 1. b   2. c   3. b   4. c

Additional Activity

Instruct students to find out more about Arthur Miller and/or *Death of a Salesman* and to give oral or written reports. Or, read more selections from the play to be acted out in class. There are many good filmed versions of this play available on videotape.

V. Body Language

Techniques

The purpose of this section is to make students aware that body language (movement and gesture) creates mood, conveys feelings, and symbolizes meaning. Remind students that body language is an important part of drama and acting. In Activity A students identify common American body language. Activity B asks students to reflect upon the proper body language in their own country/culture. Activity C should help students better understand body language in America. Remind students that within one country/culture there are different opinions about the "correct" body language. Answers given for Activity C are the (humble) opinion of the author. In Activity D, students are asked to review examples of body language in *Death of a Salesman* and to interpret meaning.

Answers

A. b = "I didn't hear you."   c = "Come here."   d = "Oh, no. I forgot" or "How stupid of me."   e = "That's great."   f = "Good luck."   g = "Stop. That's enough."   h = "I don't know."

B. Answers will vary.

C. 1.a. T b. F c. T d. F; 2. c; 3.a. T b. F c. F d. T; 4. a

D. 1. Answers will vary.   2. Linda is trying to help Willy; she treats him almost like a mother would treat a child. Willy is trying to assert himself; though weak, he continues to try to take action.   3. symbol of togetherness; happy home life; a fresh start

VI. Music

Techniques

In this section students should understand that music is frequently used to create atmosphere and setting. For Activity A, play four or five very different types of music. Encourage students to write their feelings, not to worry about grammar or spelling. If possible, play recordings of theme music from famous dramas (e.g., the movie *Jaws*) and ask students how the music creates/captures the mood of the drama. It is important to complete this section as it is used later in chapter 1, section VIII, "Writing and Acting."

VII. Stress and Tone

Techniques

In this section remind students that stress and tone convey mood and meaning. For Activity B, arrange students in pairs and let them read the dialogue aloud, without help. At first, students will not have a good understanding of the dialogue. A few *possible* interpretations are given here. In Activity C and Activity D, pairs (or small groups) use their knowledge of setting, mood, stress and tone, and so forth, to create an original interpretation of the script. Encourage pairs to be creative and remind them that the choices they make will change the meaning of the scene. Student comprehension can be checked through their performances.

Answers and Script

A.
1.   *A:* Honey, I'm home.
     B: Hello sweetie-pie. How was *your day?*
     A: Really really good. My boss was *so* happy with my work that he gave me a *raise.* It looks like we can go to *Disneyland* this summer.
     B: Disneyland! That sounds *great. But* wouldn't you *rather* go to *Rome?*
2.   *A: Hi* Mom! *What's* for *lunch?* I'm *hungry.*
     B: Well, I made *tuna* salad and *chicken* soup.
     A: Oh *Mom.* Can I have *tomato soup* instead of *chicken?*
3.   *A:* The *problem* with *you* is, you *need* to get a *normal* job.
     B: What do you *mean?* I'm an *actor.* I *live* for my *art.*
     A: Maybe you're living *for* your art, but you're *also* living on *my money!*

Additional Activity

Have the students write additional conversations and put them on the board. Then, the students should read the conversation aloud to the class. Volunteers should come up to underline the stressed words.

B. We do not know what is happening because we are not given information about characters, setting, body language, stress and tone, etc. Possibilities include two people   a. moving to a new house, country, etc.; b. about to commit suicide;   c. getting married/divorced;   d. committing a crime.

VIII. Writing and Acting

Techniques

In this section students are asked to write and act in a short drama, using many of the dramatic elements discussed earlier in the chapter. It is important to limit group size for this section so that all students must act. Students must complete Activity A before Activity B (which might also be given as a homework assignment). For Activity C, encourage students to use pictures, movement, and/or props (in addition to music) to develop their characters and setting. Do not allow students to read from notes and remind them that, for this exercise, correct grammar is *not* necessary. In my experience, performances take a long time! I have found it useful to set clear time limits (usually 30–50 minutes) for the writing and practice of the dramas. If this is impossible, the activity could be given as homework. Wrap up the chapter by discussing each "performance" using the "Postperformance Questions."

Additional Activities

1. Videotape each performance and later watch/discuss the tape with the class.
2. To motivate students, you could give each group a score based on its dramatic presentation. A suggested score sheet follows.

Performance Score Sheet

1. Length of drama   _____ (20 points)
2. Content of drama   _____ (25 points)
3. Member participation   _____ (25 points)
   (did every member of the
   group speak?)
4. Use of pictures, music,   _____ (15 points)
   props
5. Use of movement   _____ (15 points)

Total _____

Chapter 2

History of the American Theater

Opening Activity

The purpose of this warm-up is to get students thinking about the subject matter, cost, audience, theater, and purpose of plays. Arrange students in groups to discuss these questions. Neither you nor the students should be concerned if you do not have much knowledge about these topics, as they will be studied in detail throughout the chapter. At the end of the chapter, you may want to return to these questions for review.

4. Possible purposes include the following: to entertain, to explain, to instruct, to persuade, to compare/contrast, to reflect, to warn, to advise, to anger, to cause a change.

Objectives for Students

Content

Understand the historical development of the American theater

Compare, contrast, and discuss historical periods

Analyze dramatic scenes for subject matter, purpose, audience, and type of theater

Read and act out excerpts from famous plays

Write and act out a dramatic scene

Language

Reading/Writing/Structures

Scanning
Organizing information in a chart format
Understanding and identifying purpose and audience of a text
Using comparative forms of adjectives and adverbs
Recognizing antonyms
Summarizing short passages
Writing a short drama

Speaking/ Listening

Acting out a short scene

Chapter Activities

I. Historical Developments

Techniques

The purpose of this section is to give students general knowledge about the history of the American theater and of drama in the English language. Activity A is a scanning activity and warm-up for the reading. In Activity B students are introduced to the reading's difficult vocabulary. Comprehension of the reading is tested through the chart in Activity D. Activity E should be used for discussion comparing the various time periods. Activity F elicits preexisting knowledge of comparative forms. For more advanced classes, the teacher may want to add additional comparative exercises. In Activity G students should match each theater with its appropriate period.

Answers

A. 1. mystery and morality plays 2. a "mystery" 3. the (English) Renaissance 4. 1660 5. Victorian melodrama 6. to inspire anger and/or to effect change

B. 1. lower-class 2. logic 3. stupid 4. literate 5. immobile
6. plain 7. destruction 8. comic 9. unimportant
10. irreligious 11. common 12. hero 13. unrealistic

D.

Period (name/date)	Subject Matter	Purpose	Type of Theater	Audience
Medieval, 14th and 15th C. (mysteries and moralities)	religious	to teach religious lessons and to entertain	carts, wagons, movable stages, outdoor	ordinary people, villagers
Renaissance, 16th and 17th C.	tragedy, history, and comedy (revival of classic Greek and Roman drama)	to instruct and entertain	partially roofed, permanent	all social classes
The Restoration 1600s–1700s	(amoral) comedies; sexual intrigue, social snobbery, aristocratic folly	entertainment of the upper classes, attendance a way to be fashionable	roofed, ornate theaters (some small, ornate, standing pit, audience members allowed on stage)	wealthy upper classes (King Charles II and his mistresses)
Victorian melodrama 18th and 19th C.	defeat of upper-class villains, and triumph of good over evil (often sentimental)	entertainment of middle classes	larger theaters; movable scenery; indoor, artificial lighting; footlights	middle classes

Period (name/date)	Subject Matter	Purpose	Type of Theater	Audience
Modern realism, 20th C.	realistic portrayal of modern times and events	shock, challenge, and instruct the audience	many different types and sizes; university and community theaters	all social classes

E.
1. Mystery plays retell the history of the whole human race (according to the Bible). Morality plays explore humankind's spiritual journey.
2. Influenced by Greek and Roman drama, playwrights developed modern forms of tragedy, comedy, and history plays.
3. A fanatical religious group, with a great deal of influence in the English Parliament. They destroyed/burned English theaters and made it a crime to be an actor.
4. During the Restoration, theaters became fully roofed and much more ornate. The audience was largely upper class, and it was fashionable to be seen at the theater. The audience stood in a standing pit and were often allowed on stage.
5. Victorian melodrama often depicts the upper class as villainous.
6. Modern audiences come from a broad range of religious, social, and economic backgrounds. They also hold a range of opinions and beliefs.

F. Answers will vary.

G.
2. Medieval; outdoor, movable stage, town and village people, religious subject matter represented through the cross
3. Victorian; ornate theater; large, middle-class audience
4. Renaissance; partially roofed theater
5. Restoration; standing pit, audience members on the stage

Additional Activity

Have students give reports/group presentations on some aspect of their own country's drama. Some ideas for reports are as follows: history of drama in (country); summary of a typical play from (country); student's opinion of the purpose and value of the theater; types of theaters used in (country); typical audience in (country).

II. Interpreting Plays

Techniques

The selections here are examples taken from the time periods discussed in the reading "Origins of the American Theater." For Activity A, first ask volunteers to read the first two selections aloud. Then discuss the answers given in the text. Remind students that the answers provided are only one interpretation of the scenes. This activity will help students interpret meaning in the next three scenes. In Activity B, students discuss their interpretations. Try to elicit comparative forms from the students to reinforce this grammar point.

Answers

A.
Scene 3

Summary:	Two women are talking about how they hate men. One woman plans to get married to show her hatred.
Subject Matter:	Love and relationships/ marriage
Purpose:	To amuse or entertain
Audience:	Women/married people
Time Period:	Restoration

Scene 4

Summary:	A wealthy man is talking to his daughter and her friend about the value of money. The friend disagrees.
Subject Matter:	money/politics/social awareness
Purpose:	To persuade or argue a political matter
Audience:	Politically and socially conscious adults
Time Period:	Victorian (melodrama)

Scene 5

Summary:	A woman desperately tries to understand why her husband has done something awful (killed himself).
Subject Matter:	Death/tragedy
Purpose:	To reflect upon the meaning of life
Audience:	General
Time Period:	Modern realism

B. Answers will vary.

Additional Activity

For more practice in interpreting plays, ask pairs to bring in an additional short scene and perform it for the class. The other students in the class should try to interpret the scene(s).

III. Writing and Acting

Techniques

The purpose of this section is to allow students to create and act in an original scene. For Activity A, arrange students in groups and let them choose a topic. The questions in Activity B should help students narrow the topic of their scene and prepare them to write. Activity C can be given as homework. When students perform in Activity D make sure that they do not use notes. You might want to do an additional activity here on improvisation. Activity E provides opportunity for teacher and peer feedback. If possible, videotape each group's performance for later review and discussion.

Chapter 3

Drama on Stage

Opening Activity

In this chapter, the students look closely at two dramatic theater performances. This opening activity is intended to give the students some background on one of the most important theater districts in the world—New York City. Students will also learn about other famous locations in New York.

A.

Answers

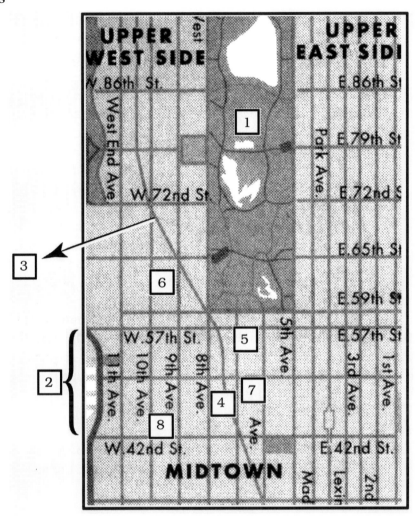

Script

New York City has hundreds of theaters, and it can be a challenge to decide where to go and what to see! A good place to start, however, is in Manhattan's Theater District, which is located between 57th and 41st Streets, just below Central Park. Find the famous street, Broadway,

Map adapted from *Fodor's 96 Pocket New York City* by Fodor's Travel Publications, Inc. © 1996 by Fodor's Travel Publications, Inc. Reprinted by permission of the publisher. Script adapted from *Let's Go: The Budget Guide to USA 1996* by Michelle C. Sullivan (New York: St. Martin's Press, 1996).

which runs diagonally through the Theater District between 6th and 8th Avenues. This street is also nicknamed "The Great White Way" because it has many brilliant lights. At the corner of Broadway and 47th Street is Duffy's Square. Here, you can find a ticket outlet that sells tickets for 25 percent to 50 percent less than the regular price on the day of performance. This is a popular service because the price of a ticket for a large Broadway show is usually at least $50.00. If you're looking for something more modern (and less expensive), try the off-Broadway theaters located between 9th and 10th Avenues on 42nd Street. This small, newly renovated district contains nine theaters, three cabarets, and many restaurants.

New York also has other exciting things besides theater. Carnegie Hall, which is located at the corner of 57th Street and 7th Avenue, is world famous for its concerts, which range from classical to contemporary. If you are in the mood for dance, check out the high-kicking Rockettes at Radio City Music Hall, located at the corner of 51st Street and 6th Avenue. If opera interests you, check out the Lincoln Center, located between 9th and 10th Avenues and West 60th and West 65th Streets.

Remember, plan ahead! To find more information about current shows, look in the Sunday newspaper edition of the *New York Times* or the magazine the *New Yorker*. You can also call the NYC/ON STAGE hotline at 212-768-1818 or an entertainment hotline that covers weekly activities at 212-360-3456.

1. T   2. F—because of its many theater lights   3. F—a ticket costs at least $50.00   4. T   5. F—it is famous for its dancers   6. T   7. F— the second number is 212-**360**-3**456.**

Additional Activity

Students should find current information about plays/theater events in the local area (if there are few choices, have students give reports on current movies). Students then give reports (written or oral) that include information about dates, prices, location, and relevant phone numbers and a brief summary of the type of drama being presented. If possible, arrange for a student field trip to see a drama. If you have access to the *New York Times* or the *New Yorker*, have students find out what plays are being featured on or off Broadway.

Objectives for Students

Content

Understand how two American plays reflect the culture of the time
Analyze two genres of plays—musicals and realism
Perform scenes from *Oklahoma!* and *A Raisin in the Sun*
Recognize and use different varieties of the English language, including
    regional speech and African-American vernacular
Write and act in a short drama that reflects your own culture

Language

Reading/Writing/Structures

Recognizing and using cohesive devices (repetition of key words, pronoun
    reference, synonyms, and linking words)
Inferring meaning from poetry
Understanding and writing similes
Combining sentences
Summarizing information for a jigsaw reading
Writing short scenes

Speaking/Listening

Listening for details
Listening for main idea
Identifying and producing regional speech and African-American
    vernacular
Acting out short scenes

I. The American Musical: *Oklahoma!*

Techniques

Activity A is a prediction and warm-up activity. Activity B is a cloze listening, and Activity C tests comprehension and allows a chance for discussion. After doing the vocabulary work in Exercise D, the students read a passage about American musicals and answer some comprehension questions in Activity E. For Activity F students are asked to *logically* arrange a full paragraph and to reflect upon that logic in Activity G. Students should recognize and label cohesive devices for Activity H. Activity I tests the students' ability to infer information. In Activities J and K, the students hear a short passage from the musical *Oklahoma!* and then try to recognize features of regional speech. Remind students that they do not need to learn all the unique characteristics of a region in order to be understood. Activity L tests students' ability to recognize and interpret regional speech, and Activity M gives them a chance to produce regional speech in a dramatic scene.

Answers

A. Answers will vary.

B.

Oh, What a Beautiful Mornin'

There's a <u>bright</u> golden haze on the <u>meadow</u>,

There's a <u>bright</u> golden haze on the <u>meadow</u>.

The corn is as <u>high</u> as an elephant's <u>eye</u>,

An' it looks like it's <u>climbing</u> clear up to the <u>sky</u>.

> *Refrain:*
>
> Oh, what a beautiful mornin',
>
> Oh, what a beautiful day.
>
> I got a beautiful feelin'
>
> Ev'rything's goin' my way.

All the <u>cattle</u> are standin' like <u>statues</u>,

All the <u>cattle</u> are standin' like <u>statues</u>.

They don't <u>turn</u> their heads as they see me <u>ride</u> by,

But a little <u>brown</u> mav'rick is <u>winking</u> her eye.

> (*refrain*)

All the <u>sounds</u> of the earth are like <u>music</u>

All the <u>sounds</u> of the earth are like <u>music</u>.

The <u>breeze</u> is so busy it don't <u>miss a</u> tree

And an ol' <u>weeping</u> willer is laughin' at me!

> (*refrain*)

Oklahoma

They couldn't pick a better time to start in life!

It ain't too early and it ain't too late

Startin' as a farmer with a brand new <u>wife</u>

Soon be living in a brand new <u>state</u>!

Brand new state

You <u>gonna</u> be great

Gonna give you barley, <u>carrots</u> and pertaters

Pasture fer the cattle

Spinach and <u>tomatoes</u>

<u>Flowers</u> on the prairie where the June bugs zoom

Plen'y of <u>air</u> and plen'y of <u>room</u>

Plen'y of room <u>to swing</u> a rope

Plen'y of <u>heart</u> and plen'y of <u>hope</u>

Oklahoma,

Where the wind comes sweepin' down the <u>plain,</u>

And the <u>waving</u> wheat

Can sure smell sweet

When the <u>wind</u> comes right behind the <u>rain</u>.

Oklahoma,

Ev'ry night my honey lamb and I

Sit <u>alone</u> and talk

And watch a <u>hawk</u>

Makin' lazy circles in the sky.

We know we <u>belong</u> to the land,

And the land we belong to is <u>grand</u>!

And when we say:

<u>Ee-ee-ow!</u>

A-yip-I-o-ee-ay!

We're only sayin',

"You're <u>doing fine</u>, Oklahoma!

Oklahoma, O.K.!

(*repeat* second half)

C.   Possible answers include the following.

	Beautiful Mornin'	*Oklahoma*
What is being "loved" in this song?	land; morning; meadow	land; Oklahoma
What is the mood of this song (peaceful, angry)?	happy; content	optimistic; excited
Why do you think this song is popular with American audiences?	Answers will vary.	Answers will vary.
Would people in your country enjoy this song? Explain.	Answers will vary.	Answers will vary.

D.   1. e   2. g   3. c   4. j   5. a   6. d   7. k   8. h   9. b   10. f   11. i

E.
1. Early musical comedy provided cheap entertainment for businesspeople and townsfolk. Though humorous, it contained little structure or plot.
2. Writers began to use a combination of American history, language, values, and beliefs to create drama with both meaning and message.
3. It combined American history, language, dance, and humor with structured and meaningful dramatic form. It also broke all preexisting records at the box office.

F.   a. 2   b. 6   c. 8   d. 1   e. 7   f. 5   g. 3   h. 9   i. 4

G. Students should note the *cohesive devices:* repetition of key words, pronoun reference, synonyms, and linking words.

H.

1. *Oklahoma!* is set in Native American territory in about 1907, the year that it officially became a state. (pronoun reference)
2. In the beginning of the musical, two of the main characters (the villainous Jud and heroic Curly) ask the same woman (Laurey) to a picnic. (synonym)
3. Laurey foolishly agrees to go with Jud, even though she really loves Curly. (linking words; pronoun reference)
4. At the picnic, however, Laurey regrets this decision and admits that she actually hates Jud and never wants to see him again. (linking word; synonym; pronoun reference)
5. As a consequence of Laurey's admission, Jud decides to kill Curly. (linking word; synonym)
6. The two men fight, and, as a result, Jud is killed. (linking words)
7. Though Curly claims that Jud's death was accidental, he is sent to trial for murder. (linking word; pronoun reference)
8. However, the judge decides that Curly did not murder Jud and sets him free. (linking word; repetition of key word; pronoun reference)
9. Finally, Laurey and Curly are free to be married and start their new life together. (linking word; pronoun reference)

I. Possible answers include the following.

1. Yes (They are truly in love.)
2. Yes (They are very excited to be living in "a brand new state.")
3. Laurey and Curly will live in a farmhouse or on a cattle ranch (as they have in the past).
4. Laurey will be a housewife, and Curly will be a cowman (cowboy) or a farmer. (Laurey will take the traditional woman's role, and Curly will continue to do the only job he apparently knows.)

K.

Pronunciation	a-tall = at all; fer = for; git = get; yere = here; purty = pretty; pitcher = picture; 'at = that; sich = such; 'at = that; c'n = can
Grammar	ain't = isn't
Vocabulary/Idioms	she don't take to me = she doesn't like me; looky here = look here; uppity = stuck-up; pay no heed = pay no attention

L. 2. that's   3. somebody likes you if they are "stuck on you"   4. going
5. fellow (man)   6. I think so.   7. what   8. everybody   9. expect
10. maybe   11. are not   12. like flying insects   13. cannot (can't)
14. are

II. Realism: *A Raisin in the Sun*

Techniques

Use Activity A to discuss and review information learned in chapters 1 and
2 and as a simple prediction. For Activity B, students try to interpret the
meaning and mood of the poem "Harlem (A Dream Deferred)." Inform students
that Langston Hughes and Lorraine Hansberry were peers and that
this poem was a direct inspiration for *A Raisin in the Sun*. Students also are
asked to find the comparisons (similes) in the poem and then work further
with similes in Activities C and D. In Activity E, students read a brief background
of *A Raisin in the Sun* and try to recognize the techniques used for
sentence combining. In Activity F, they then use these techniques to recombine
sentences that describe the central characters and conflict of the play.
In the remaining activities in the chapter, the students read excerpts from
the play and identify the characters, situation, mood, and African-
American vernacular used in each excerpt. The activity is set up as a jigsaw
reading. After each group has completed its section of the chart, have them
perform for and "teach" the rest of the class. By the end of the activity all
students should have a completed chart.

Answers and Handouts

A.   The plot, characters, setting, language, props, and so on, are as real as
possible (not idealized or made humorous as in *Oklahoma!*). Subject
matter is taken from everyday life and often reflects problems faced by
common people.

B.
1.   a dream that has been postponed or delayed
2.   serious; solemn; angry
3.   b. fester like a sore   c. stink like rotten meat   d. crust and sugar over
like a syrupy sweet   e. sag like a heavy load   f. explode

C.
1.   <u>Your voice</u> is like <u>sunshine on a rainy day</u>./refreshing; beautiful
2.   <u>She's</u> as <u>big as a horse</u>./large; fat
3.   <u>My car</u> is as <u>rusty as an old nail</u>./rusty

4. After spilling coffee on her boss, <u>Mary</u> looked <u>like a ripe tomato.</u>/red; embarrassed
5. <u>Her eyes</u> are as <u>blue as the sea.</u>/very blue
6. <u>My brother</u> is as smart as <u>Einstein.</u>/very smart
7. <u>Her lips</u> are <u>like cherries.</u>/red; pretty
8. <u>I'</u>m as <u>busy as a bee in summertime.</u>/very busy

D. Possible answers include the following.

1. My teacher is as thin as a nail.
2. My classmate is as dumb as an elephant.
3. He drives like my grandmother.
4. This kitchen floor looks like a sparkling diamond.
5. This classroom is as hot as a desert.

E.

Coordinating conjunction	and
Conjunctive adverb	As a result
Adverb clause	because it discusses real problems faced by many minorities in American society
Relative (adjective) clause	which was an immediate success on Broadway
Adverbial or adjectival participial clause	Written by Lorraine Hansberry

F. Possible answers include the following.

1. After her husband, Big Walter, died, Mama received a $10,000 insurance check.
2. Mama is troubled and upset by the money, because everyone in the family wants to use the money differently.
3. Mama, who is over 60 years old, has a simple dream of owning a house with a garden.
4. Walter Lee, who is 35 years old and Mama's son, wants the money to open a liquor store in order to be financially independent.
5. Walter Lee's tired wife, Ruth, who is pregnant and working as a maid, wants the money for a new home for herself and her growing family.

6. Travis, who is 10 years old, is the son of Ruth and Walter Lee.
7. Studying to become a medical doctor, Mama's intelligent daughter, Beneatha, wants the money to pay her tuition bills and complete school.

G. See the completed chart in Activity J.

H.
1. It isn't much. (*use of* "ain't")
2. There isn't anything as precious to me. (*overuse of negative*)
3. Any penny that comes out of it or goes in it is for you to look after. (*absence of -s suffix for third person singular*)
4. Be the head of this family from now on like you are supposed to be. (*absence of forms of* "to be")

I. See the chart in Activity J. Students may find additional examples of African-American vernacular that are not discussed in the box (for example, the omission of articles and the frequent use of "got to" for have to). An exhaustive definition of African-American vernacular is beyond the scope of this section. See Paul Stoller (ed.), *Black American English* (New York: Delta Publishing, 1975) as a good reference if you wish to discuss this in more detail.

J.

	Excerpt #1	*Excerpt #2*	*Excerpt #3*	*Excerpt #4*
Characters	Mama (Walter)	Ruth and Walter	Mama and Beneatha	Mama, Ruth, and Travis
Summary of situation	Mama apologizes to Walter; asks Walter to be the head of the family.	Walter discusses his frustrations; becomes angry at Ruth because all she cares about is whether or not he eats his eggs.	Beneatha reveals her dream and her disbelief in God; Mama is shocked.	Mama and Ruth celebrate; Travis is given hope.

	Excerpt #1	*Excerpt #2*	*Excerpt #3*	*Excerpt #4*
Mood	serious, angry	tense, angry	proud, determined	hopeful
African-American vernacular	like you supposed to be (1); that I been doing to you (2); ain't got nothing (3, 6); come out of it (5); It ain't much (6)	I been married eleven years (2); You never say nothing new (3); That ain't none of our money (3, 6)	'Course you going to be a doctor, honey (1); It don't sound nice for a young girl (5)	you glad about the house? (1); cause it was him who give you the house (5); which ain't now or never was no kitchen (3, 6)

Handouts

Three handouts follow. Their use is discussed in Activity J of the student book.

Excerpt #2 (from act I, scene 1)

Ruth: Walter . . . Eat your eggs, they gonna be cold.

Walter: *(Straightening up from her and looking off)* That's it. There you are. Man says to his woman: I got me a dream. His woman say: Eat your eggs. *(Sadly, but gaining in power)* Man say: I got to take hold of this here world, baby! And a woman will say: Eat your eggs and go to work. *(Passionately now)* Man say: I got to change my life, I'm choking to death, baby! And his woman say—*(in utter anguish as he brings his fists down on his thighs)*—Your eggs is getting cold!

Ruth: *(Softly)* Walter, that ain't none of our money.

Walter: *(Not listening at all or even looking at her)* This morning, I was lookin' in the mirror and thinking about it . . . I'm thirty-five years old; I been married eleven years and I got a boy who sleeps in the living room—*(Very, very quietly)* and all I got to give him is stories about how rich white people live . . .

Ruth: Eat your eggs, Walter.

Walter: *(Slams the table and jumps up)* DAMN MY EGGS . . . DAMN ALL THE EGGS THAT EVER WAS!

Ruth: Then go to work.

Walter: *(Looking up at her)* See—I'm trying to talk to you 'bout myself—*(Shaking his head with repetition)*—and all you can say is eat them eggs and go to work.

Ruth: *(Wearily)* Honey, you never say nothing new. I listen to you every day, every night and every morning, and you never say nothing new. *(Shrugging)* So you would rather BE Mr. Arnold than be his chauffeur. So—I would *rather* be living in Buckingham Palace.

Excerpt # 3 (from act I, scene 1)

Beneatha: . . . I am going to be a doctor and everybody around here better understand that!

Mama: (Kindly) 'Course you going to be a doctor, honey, God willing.

Beneatha: (Drily) God hasn't got a thing to do with it.

Mama: Beneatha—that just wasn't necessary.

Beneatha: Well—neither is God. I get sick of hearing about God.

Mama: Beneatha!

Beneatha: I mean it! I'm just sick and tired of hearing about God all the time. What has He got to do with anything? Does He pay tuition?

Mama: You 'bout to get your fresh little jaw slapped!

Beneatha: Why? Why can't I say what I want to around here, like everybody else?

Mama: It don't sound nice for a young girl to say things like that— you wasn't brought up that way. Me and your father went to trouble to get you and Brother to church every Sunday.

Beneatha: Mama, you don't understand. It's all a matter of ideas, and God is just one idea I don't accept. It's not important. I am not going out and be immoral or commit crimes because I don't believe in God. I don't even think about it. It's just that I get tired of Him getting credit for all the things the human race achieves through its own stubborn effort. There simply is no blasted God—there is only man and it is he who makes miracles!
(Mama listens, rises slowly, and powerfully slaps Beneatha's face)

Mama: Now—you say after me, in my mother's house there is still God. In my mother's house there is still God.

Excerpt #4 (from act II, scene 1)

Mama: *(Holding out her hands to her grandson)* Well—at least let me tell
        him something. I want him to be the first to hear . . . Come
        here Travis—*(She takes him by the shoulder and looks into his
        face)*—you know that money we got in the mail that morning?

Travis: Yes'm—

Mama: Well—what you think your grandmama gone and done with
        that money?

Travis: I don't know, Grandmama.

Mama: *(Putting her finger on his nose for emphasis)* She went out and
        bought you a house! *(. . . explosion comes from Walter, who
        turns away. Mama continues to Travis.)* You glad about the
        house? It's going to be yours when you get to be a man.

Travis: Yeah—I always wanted to live in a house.

Mama: All right, gimme some sugar then—*(Travis embraces her.)* Now
        when you say your prayers tonight, you thank God and your
        grandfather—'cause it was him who give you the house—in his
        way. *(Travis is sent to bed, and Mama and Ruth discuss the
        new house.)*

Ruth: . . . So you went and did it!

Mama: Yes, I did. . .

Ruth: *(Struck senseless with the news, . . . she sits a moment, her fists
        propping her chin in thought, and then she starts to rise,
        bringing her fists down with vigor . . .)* Well—well—All I can say
        is—if this is my time in life—MY TIME—to say good-bye—*(And
        she builds with momentum as she starts to circle the room . . .)*—
        to these Goddamned cracking walls!—*(She pounds the walls)*—
        and these marching roaches!—and this cramped little closet

which ain't now or never was no kitchen! . . . then I say it loud and good, HALLELUJAH! AND GOOD-BYE MISERY . . . I DON'T NEVER WANT TO SEE YOUR UGLY FACE AGAIN! *(She laughs joyously and flings her arms up in the air)* Lena?

Mama: *(Moved, watching her happiness)* Yes, honey?

Ruth: *(Looking off)* Is there—is there a whole lot of sunlight?

Mama: *(Understanding)* Yes, child, there's a whole lot of sunlight.

K.

1. no
2. no
3. In Excerpt #1, she gives some money to Walter Lee. In Excerpt #4, she uses it to buy a house.
4. 'Course you going to be a doctor, honey; you glad about the house?

L. In the actual play, Walter Lee gives the money Mama gave him to a friend who takes the money and runs. We don't know if Beneatha goes to medical school or if Mama will be happy in her new home. It is hinted at in the play, however, that they will be heavily discriminated against in their new home.

III. Writing and Acting

Techniques

The purpose of this section is to give closure to the chapter by asking students to reflect on some aspect of their culture and how it can be shown through a dramatic performance.

Chapter 4

Drama on the Radio

Opening Activity

Tell students that these exercises are used regularly by professional actors to improve speech and pronunciation. They focus on body and facial relaxation, correct posture, breathing, articulation, tone, pitch, rhythm, projection, stress, and intonation and can be repeated as often as necessary (students may do them at home) until students feel comfortable. For exercise 3, the class should read the poem aloud, clapping out the rhythm. Go over any necessary vocabulary. The class should then continue clapping out the rhythm, but individual students should take turns reading each sentence of the poem.

Answers and Script

1. *Face and Body Relaxation*

Stand up straight, legs slightly apart, shoulders relaxed, looking straight ahead. Slowly rotate your head four times to the left and four times to the right. Roll your right shoulder back four times and then do the same with your left shoulder. Repeat this action but roll your shoulders forward. Finally, roll both shoulders together (front and back) eight times. Inhale deeply while stretching your hands high above your head. Keeping both arms above your head, reach for the ceiling five times with your left hand and five times with your right. Exhale deeply as you slowly lower your arms to your sides. Shake out the remaining tension in your body for at least 30 seconds.

2. *Breathing and Tone*
   1. Count aloud as far as possible on one breath.
   2. Take a normal breath and gradually expend it saying, "HMMM." Repeat this three times. Repeat this exercise but say "MA," "NOOO," "HIII," "YOUUUU," "LAYYYY," "FREEE."
   3. Repeat the words *rhythm, moan, scene,* and *love,* focusing on the final consonant sound.
   4. Stand erect, hands on your hips, and then suddenly draw in your breath through your mouth as if you were greatly frightened. Locate and note the action of the breathing muscles. Repeat several times.
   5. Focus on your breathing muscles while shouting a single word like *Stop, Yes,* or *No* as many times as possible in one breath.

Additional Activity

Ask students to recite their favorite short poems in class. As each student reads, ask the other students to listen for and tap out the rhythm.

Objectives for Students

Content

Describe the development of radio in America

Understand and describe connections between American radio and culture

Understand the importance of sound and emotion in radio drama

Act out a popular radio drama

Write a short radio drama

Language

Reading/Writing/Structure

Interpreting simple graphs

Using nouns, verbs, adjectives, and adverbs in sentences describing increase and decrease

Predicting the conclusion to a text

Writing cause-effect sentences

Writing a short radio drama

Speaking/Listening

Using facial and body relaxation
Practicing breathing, rhythm, and tone
Articulating and projecting speech
Listening for and producing sounds for a passage
Listening for specific sounds and emotions
Speaking with emotion
Acting out a short drama

Chapter Activities

I. Development of American Radio

Techniques

In this section, students become familiar with basic terms and facts about the growth of American radio and describe them using words of increase and decrease and cause-effect statements. For Activity A, encourage students to describe the graph using as many different nouns, verbs, adjectives, and adverbs as possible. Activity D tests reading comprehension.

Answers

A. Possible answers include the following.

1. The use of radios increased dramatically and the cost decreased slightly.
2. The cost fell while the use of radios rose.
3. There was a steady climb in the use of radios and a decline in the cost.
4. There was a slight increase in the use of radios and an increase in the cost.
5. The gradual increase in the use of radios continued, but there was a sharp drop in the cost.
6. From 1925 to 1930, the cost declined slightly. From 1930 to 1940, the cost fell even further. After a slight rise in cost between 1940 and 1945, the cost declined somewhat sharply between 1945 and 1950. The use of radios increased sharply from 1925 to 1930 and then continued steadily climbing until 1950. In general, costs decreased and ownership increased for the entire time period.

C.
cause *(led to)*
effect *(was caused by)*

D. Possible answers include the following.

1. The development of alternating current power, the fact that radios were manufactured and sold in stores, and the idea of radio as a cheap form of entertainment during the depression led to an increase in radio use.
2. The decrease in the cost of radios was the result of the increase in manufacturing. Radio use continued to increase due to the increase in the number and variety of channels.
3. The ability to get "on the spot" coverage of WWII led to an even greater increase in radio use.

Additional Activity

Ask students to collect data on a topic that interests them (e.g., the number of foreign students studying at U.S. universities). Students should arrange data into graphs, which can then be presented to the teacher or class.

II. Theater of the Mind

Techniques

Activity A should review the concept of a golden age and warm up students for the text "Theater of the Mind." Questions 1–3 in Activity C provide a comprehension check for the reading. Make sure students understand the meaning of a "verbal definition," as they will need to produce these in the next section. Question 4 reviews the characteristics of dramatic form (from chap. 1).

Answers

A. Answers will vary.

C.
1. 1930–53
2. through a combination of sound and imagination
3. a phrase or a sentence written to describe a sound or setting: "Listen to that rain!"; "Here come two men on horses!"

4. Melodrama. Soap operas usually contain exaggerated and unbelievable story lines and incredibly good and incredibly evil characters. They are also fictitious.

III. Sound and Radio

Techniques

In this section students will recognize and produce sound in radio drama. Students must be able to recognize and produce verbal definitions. Activity A is a warm-up listening exercise. For Activity B, arrange students in small groups. One student reads aloud, while other students (the audience) supply the appropriate sounds. For Activity C, group students and let them write a short drama, *including* sound directions. Collect the finished dramas and let each group perform *without* using the sound directions that they have written. It is up to the rest of the class to supply the sound for each performance. Performers must then check their sound directions (and verbal definitions) to see if they match the sounds produced by the audience. You may have to remind students that this is *radio* drama and they must not use gesture to convey meaning. If possible, tape-record students' work so they can later correct and edit their speech.

Answers/Script

A.

Chicago Morning

It was a cold winter morning in Chicago. Paul was sound asleep in his warm bed. Outside the strong northeast wind blew (*) across the lake, and the window shutters beat rhythmically (*) against the house. Suddenly, the radio alarm went off (*). From a distant room, the phone rang (*). Sleepy Paul sat up quickly in bed, yawned (*), and stretched. Then he jumped up and hit the radio alarm clock.(*) He looked out the windows and heard a train (*), and, in the distance, the sound of a fire engine bell (*). Again the phone rang (*), and he stumbled across the room, bumping his leg on the bed as he went (*) and scaring his dog (*). He picked up the phone and said, "Hello" (*). But no one answered. All he heard was a low and dull dial tone. (*) Paul slammed down the phone (*) and prepared himself for another day in the city.

B. Answers will vary.

IV. Language and Emotion

Techniques

This section reinforces the idea that emotion is expressed through tone, stress, and intonation. It also serves as a warm-up for the dramatization in section V of this chapter. Activity A should illustrate to students that the *same* words can express *different* meaning. Activity B gives students the opportunity to speak with emotion. Activity C is a vocabulary building exercise and might be done as homework. Students should use the vocabulary list from Activity C to read the sentences in Activity D. Encourage students to exaggerate their speech to make their emotions clear to the class.

Answers and Text

A.

First ring: "Hello, who is this?" *(normal, friendly voice)*

Second ring: "Hello, who is this?" *(beginning to get annoyed, suspicious)*

Third ring: "Hello, who is this?" *(clearly angry, upset)*

Depending on the tone of voice, the *same* words can convey very different meanings.

C.   *Possible examples:* happy, sad, bored, calmly, depressed, eagerly, frustrated, gleefully, hurt, intensely, joyfully, lovingly, meanly, openly, patiently, questioning, rudely, stately, thoughtfully, uppity, vainly, wishfully

D.   Answers will vary.

V. Dramatization: *The Shadow*

Techniques

In this section students listen to part of an episode from the popular radio drama, *The Shadow*. Remind students that to be successful, they will have to put much of what they have learned/practiced in chapter 4 into actual use. In Activity A, the students hear the introduction that is heard in all of the radio performances of *The Shadow*, in order to get a feel for its somewhat "sinister" or "frightening" nature. For Activity B, students listen for the main idea of the opening scene of the episode "Poison Death." In Activity C, students learn more about the radio drama, and about what happens in the episode prior to the final scene. The remaining activities in the chapter revolve around this final scene. In Activity D, students listen and read along to the scene. They are then asked to answer some comprehension questions in Activity E. In order to answer these questions, the students can either look back at the written scene, or the teacher can play the scene again. In Activity F, the students listen a final time to the scene and are asked to listen for the emotions being expressed by the actors, as well as identify the sound that they hear. Before doing this activity, it might help to review some of the vocabulary words pertaining to emotions that they learned in the previous section. This activity would also lend itself to having students use a thesaurus to find a variety of words related to a particular emotion.

Answers and Script

A. Answers will vary.

B. A number of people have been mysteriously poisoned, and some have been murdered.

(*sounds:* music, ringing telephone)

Man: Mercy hospital.

Woman: Quick! Send an ambulance to 217 Shoreview Road. My children, they're poisoned, dying! Oh hurry, hurry please, hurry! (*sound:* music)

Woman: Doctor, doctor, what's wrong with my husband?

Doctor: He's been poisoned.

Woman;   Poisoned? Isn't there something you can do? Some way of saving him?

Doctor: No, I'm sorry my dear. It's too late. Your husband is dead. (*sounds:* music, emergency vehicle bells)

Man: What's this Bill? Another poison case?

Bill: Yes. The calls are coming in faster than we can answer them.

Man: Well this one will have to go to General. The emergency ward is full. Not a cop left.

Bill: The same thing in every hospital in town. They're swamped, all poison cases. And nobody knows how they're getting it or what it is. (*sound:* music)

C.
1. Lamont Cranston; Margot Lane
2. The fact that he could become invisible so as to battle dangerous criminals and fight injustices.
3. The Shadow uses some kind of mental trick to shut down or turn off a part of the person's brain.
4. The radio program appealed to a wide American audience from all social and economic classes.
5. melodrama
6. The first note threatens that either a million dollars be paid in ransom, or a million people will be killed. The second note singles out one man to be killed, David Brinkley, chief of the department of sanitation.
7. Because the notes have been signed the Shadow.
8. A. D. Gerber is the criminal. He is angry because he does not have the job he wants.
9. Answers will vary.

E.
1. He means he thought that he had previously killed the Shadow with the acid.
2. His revenge, for not having the job as chief of the city's sanitation department.
3. The blood marks in the snow.
4. Throw him off the tower, or take him with him if he jumps himself.
5. So that everyone knows that it wasn't really him that signed the notes. If the criminal hadn't used the Shadow's name in the ransom notes, he wouldn't have felt the need to be "vindicated."

F.

Gerber:	**(frightened, startled)** Who's that?
Shadow:	The man you thought you'd left in your laboratory. Burnt and blind with acid. The Shadow!
Gerber:	Yes? But I thought I had you! Well, all right! Keep on following me. You're a long way behind me by the sound of your voice.

(*sound:* **walking up stairs**)

Shadow:	Yes. Yes, but you have to stop when you get to the top. And I shall catch up with you.
Gerber:	Ha ha! Yes. But by that time I shall have poisoned the water.
Shadow:	You forget the trap door to the tank may be locked.
Gerber:	It will be rusty and easy to break.
Shadow:	But it will take time, and I shall be gaining on you. You need to hurry, Gerber! It's too bad you missed my face with that acid, isn't it Gerber?
Gerber:	Yes, but some of it went on you. (laughter) I heard it sizzling in your flesh.
Shadow:	On my hands, that's all. Don't you want to see them?
Gerber:	Then you must be suffering holding on to the ice covered ladder!
Shadow:	Not as much as you'll suffer once I reach you!
Gerber:	All right. Hurry Shadow! I'm on the top already. You were right, Shadow. The trap door is locked. But that won't stop me. I'm going to blow it open with my revolver.

(*sound:* **gunshot**)
Oh! The lock is broken Shadow. You'd better hurry up.

Shadow:	I'm not far below you now, Gerber.
Gerber:	Now I'm opening the trap door Shadow.
Shadow:	Yes, yes, I hear it, Gerber. But you'll never put the poison in the water.

The Shadow from Condé Nast Publications, Inc.

Gerber: I have the bottle in my hand. I'm pulling out the stopper!

Shadow: **(angry, incensed, irate, mad, furious)** And I'm here to knock it out of your hands!
(*sound:* a bottle being knocked out of Gerber's hand onto the floor)

Gerber: You broke it! You spilled the poison! You've spoiled my revenge—you spoiled it! But you'll pay for it. You're leaving blood marks on the snow with your hands. You can't get off the top of this tower! You can't get past me to the ladder. I don't need to see you to find you. The blood marks will show me where you are.

Shadow: Come and get me, Gerber. I'm waiting for you here on top of the tank.

Gerber: I know you are. And you can't go any further, or you'll slip and fall to the ground, hundreds of feet below!

Shadow: **(confident, assured, secure)** Don't be so sure, Gerber.

Gerber: There. There, I touched you, Shadow. You squirm very cleverly. But I've got you. I've got hold of you. You won't get away from me, Shadow.
(*sound:* **police vehicle sirens**)

Shadow: And you won't get away from the police. Hear them coming?

Gerber: You, you warned the police!

Shadow: Yes.

Gerber: But before they get here, I'm going to throw you off the tower, Shadow!

Shadow: You might fall off yourself if you try to do that.

Gerber: If I do, I'll pull you off with me!
(*sounds:* **scuffling, police vehicle sirens**)

Westin: Silence, silence. There's somebody on top of that water tower. Bring your searchlight up there quick.

Policeman 1: Right, Commissioner Westin.

Shadow: It's Commissioner Westin. He's come to take you himself, Gerber. You should feel honored.

Gerber:	**(worried, distressed, alarmed, fearful, nervous)** He'll never get me! He'll never take me alive!
Policeman 1:	There he is, Commissioner. Right on the top. He appears to be struggling with somebody.
Westin:	Get the searchlight on him. Hold it.
Shadow:	You're caught, Gerber. You're trapped, you're trapped. There's no escape, Gerber!
Gerber:	Listen! Listen to me, Commissioner Westin. You'll never get me! Never! I did it! I killed all those people. I made you think it was the Shadow!
Policeman 1:	Get back, Commissioner. He's trying to jump!
Shadow:	**(concerned, affected, tender, moved)** You'll be killed, Gerber.
Gerber:	I'm not afraid. I'm not afraid! Because you're coming with me, Shadow. Come on, Shadow! Come with me! Come with me! (*sound:* **screaming and a thump as the body hits the ground**)
Sergeant:	**(stunned, shocked, astonished)** He did it! He jumped!
Westin:	Throw your light over there to the foot of the tower. See who it is! That's our man, the poisoner.
Policeman:	There's the body.
Sergeant:	Yeah, he must be dead as a doornail.
Westin:	Yes, no man could fall that distance and live. Turn him over. Let's see his face.
Sergeant:	He's dead alright. Neck's broken. Why it's . . .
Westin:	**(surprised, bewildered, incredulous)** Why it's Gerber! Gerber! The chief chemist of the sanitation department. Who would ever have thought a man in his position. . . .
Sergeant:	He was struggling with someone up there on the top of the tower. Where's the other man?
Westin:	Look around at the base of the tower. See if you can find another body. Look in the bushes.

Sergeant: I suppose we could have missed him, but I don't see how.

Westin: Can't see a thing in these snow flurries! Swing the searchlight around. Anything over there, Sergeant?

Sergeant: No, no sign.

Policeman 1:   No, I don't see anybody here, Sergeant!

Policeman 2:   Nobody over here either.

Policeman 3:   Nothin' over on this side.
(*sound:* **footsteps**)

Westin: Listen!
(*sound:* laughter)

Westin: Shadow?

Shadow: **(calm, serene, tranquil, composed)** Yes, Commissioner Westin. The Shadow. I am walking down. And Commissioner, don't bother to search anymore. I am the man Gerber was struggling with up on the tower.

Westin: So you trapped Gerber?

Shadow: Yes, Commissioner. I trapped him. Gerber's your man. The man who tried to poison the people of this city . . . into paying him a half a million dollars.

Westin: Well, he won't poison anymore by the looks of him.

Shadow: And now, would you do something for me, Commissioner?

Westin: By all means.

Shadow: If you don't mind, Commissioner, I'd like to publicly take the credit for solving this mystery. Gerber committed his crimes in the name of the Shadow. And I . . . I rather think the real Shadow deserves to be vindicated, don't you?
(*sound:* **music**)

Chapter 5

Drama on Television

Opening Activity

These exercises are similar to the introduction exercises in chapter 4, "Drama on the Radio." They are meant to warm up students and to illustrate the importance of *facial expressions* and *reactions* in television dramas. For exercise 1, stress that students should not make any noise but should try to communicate their sentences by clearly mouthing out each word. For exercises 2 and 3, have several students take turns sitting in a chair facing the rest of the class. Let the class decide whether the student in the chair is able to successfully express his or her reactions using only facial expressions.

Objectives for Students

Understand the concept of television drama and differentiate it from
    other forms of drama
Direct a television scene with appropriate camera angles and face and
    body movements
Understand the predominance of television in American society
Survey people about their television viewing habits
Describe genres of television programming and the concept of prime time
Analyze television ratings and understand how they are calculated
Act out an authentic television drama

Language

Reading/Writing/Structures

Guessing vocabulary and idiomatic expressions from the surrounding
   context
Writing a questionnaire to survey people about their television habits
Editing for subject-verb agreement
Predicting and writing the next scene of a television drama

Speaking/Listening

Understanding language clues in the introduction to a lecture
Surveying people about their television habits
Presenting the results of a survey
Paraphrasing ideas from a text
Performing a television drama with appropriate tone, stress, emotion,
   and body movements

Chapter Activities

I. Television Drama

Techniques

The purpose of this section is to illustrate ways in which television drama is
different from other forms of drama, particularly in the theater. In this
section, students also identify basic television camera angles and have the
opportunity to practice using these angles in original ways. Though possible answers are given, students should not be worried if they cannot fully
answer Activity A. You might, however, return to this exercise after com-
pleting this section. Activity B serves as a warm-up to a lecture on television
drama and asks students to use contextual clues to guess the meanings of
words that will appear in the lecture. In Activity C, students listen to the
introduction of the lecture to see if they can identify the purpose and organization of the lecture. Students should take notes in Activity D and are
encouraged to use their prior knowledge of note-taking symbols and abbreviations. The students then use their notes to answer the comprehension
questions in Activity E. In Activity F, students are asked to match pictures
that show various camera angles to the names of those angles and then to
add those types of camera angles to a written scene in Activity G. If possible,
have groups videotape their performances. Activity H can be done as homework or in class.

Answers

A. Possible answers include the following.

Time limitations: A typical play might be two hours, interrupted only by one short intermission, whereas a typical television show is only 30–60 minutes, interrupted by many commercial advertisements.

Setting: It is easier to produce a very distant past (e.g., the Middle Ages) or the future on television, and the result is more likely to be realistic. The setting can also change much more easily.

Character and plot: Character and plot development must be rapid in television, and plots are often more "action-packed." Also, unlike in a play, which is usually written for a specific audience, the characters and plot of a typical television program must have a very wide appeal.

Audience: The audience of a typical television program will be larger and more diverse.

Acting: It is easier for small actions/facial expressions to be conveyed through television. Television cameras can also focus in on particular details, especially on the reactions of actors.

B. 1. changed 2. keep (to) 3. parts 4. disparate or varied
5. diversions

C.

Today we will look at how television drama is unique by comparing it to drama in the theater in four principal areas: time limitations, subject matter and audience, character and plot development, and how actors act and react.

D.

Script

Television Drama

Quite simply, television drama is one of the most powerful and influential forms of drama in the modern world. Unlike in other forms of drama, we can realistically travel through time, place, and even space through television in a way that no other generation could have imagined. We are also able to step more directly into the private lives of individuals, analyzing their successes, failures, and secret desires—without ever leaving our own living rooms. Today we will look at how television drama is unique by comparing it to drama in the theater in four principal areas: time limitations, subject matter and audience, character and plot development, and how actors act and react.

The first major difference is with regard to time limitations. The length of an actor's speech, or of an entire theater play, may be altered by the director in order to produce a particular meaning or feeling in the audience. On the other hand, a television drama is severely restricted by time. Television shows must adhere exactly to a prescribed 30–60 minute time period, so that all paid advertisements will be seen and so that the next scheduled show will begin on time. TV shows are also normally broken up into 10–20 minute segments, separated by a large number of commercials. Indeed, the average television viewer sees over 22,000 commercial advertisements each year. Each segment must be carefully scripted to ensure that the audience will not change channels during the "commercial break."

A second major difference has to do with subject matter and audience. While a few thousand people may choose to go to a particular theater play, a drama on television will be seen by millions. As a result, the subject matter of most television shows must appeal to an extremely large and diverse audience. Because television writers know that their audience will consist of people of all ages, races, socioeconomic backgrounds, and interests, it is important that they are able to create dramas which have universal themes and appeal.

Character and plot development are also different on television. In contrast to the quiet and dark atmosphere of a theater, television is viewed at home in an atmosphere full of distractions. Television writers know that, at any given moment, the audience could be talking to someone else, answering a knock on the door, or, worst of all, checking to see what's on another channel. As a result, television dramas often contain extremely rapid character and plot development, as well as action-packed, tense situations.

A final difference between television and theater drama is in the acting and reacting of the actors. Actors in the theater must learn how to project their voices loudly and clearly and to develop their characters through body movements and gesture. But the same loud speaking voice or grand gesture which looks natural on a large stage will probably look overdone and foolish on TV. Television actors, therefore, concentrate much less on vocal projection and more on "naturalness of expression." Furthermore, the sophisticated use of lighting and camera angles has resulted in much of television acting being done only from "the neck up." This means that television actors must work very hard to make their facial expressions seem realistic and convincing.

Not only do actors in television need to act differently, but they also need to learn how to react. In a typical theater production, the audience's attention is focused on the actor who is speaking and/or moving. In television, however, focus is often on the reactions of the other actors, rather than the actor who is speaking. In a scene with a reaction shot, then, we might hear an actor saying the words, "Julie, your father is dead," but while we are hearing these words, the camera will be focused only on the face of Julie.

E.
1. Television shows must adhere exactly to a prescribed 30–60 minute time period, so that all paid advertisements will be seen and so that the next scheduled show will begin on time.
2. 22,000
3. A television audience is usually much more diverse.
4. Television writers know that, at any given moment, the audience could be talking to someone else, answering a knock on the door, or, worst of all, checking to see what's on another channel. In other words, there are many distractions.
5. Acting on television must be more natural than acting in the theater, and more emphasis is placed on the reactions of actors.

F. a. 2 b. 4 c. 1 d. 7 e. 3 f. 5 g. 6

G./H. Answers will vary.

II. The Predominance of Television

Techniques

In this section students are introduced to the overwhelming predominance of television in society. In Activity A, students decide if statistics about television use are actually higher or lower than those stated. They then listen to a lecture to check their guesses. They must listen carefully to the numbers given and write the correct statistic above the incorrect statistic provided (Activity B). In Activity C, the students are asked to reflect on their own television viewing habits, and they then work in groups in Activity D to develop a questionnaire to survey others about their television viewing habits. Students are then asked to give oral presentations based on their findings. You may want to supplement this activity with further instruction on how to give an oral presentation or how to prepare charts, graphs, and so on, on the computer.

Answers

A.   Answers will vary.

B.
1.   The number of homes with televisions went from *4.6 million* to 94.2 million from 1950 to 1994.
2.   The average number of television viewing hours per day in 1980 was *6.73* hours.
3.   Women watch the most television daily, with an average of *4.42 hours* per day.
4.   Children between 1 and 2 years of age watch an average of *2 hours per day.*
5.   In one year the average child watches *1,300 hours* of television.
6.   *50%* of children between ages 6 and 17 have a TV set in their bedroom.

Script

The Predominance of Television

Good afternoon. Today we're going to look at one of the most influential media—television. Most of you have grown up with television; you don't remember a time without television in your lives. But perhaps you're not aware of the scope of the influence television has had in the average American's life.

Consider this: In 1950 only 4.6 million homes in America had a television. In 1994, however, the number had reached 94.2 million homes with televisions. When you consider that the number of homes with televisions in the U.S. is 98 percent of the population, you can see that Americans consider television an integral item in their households.

But ownership only tells a small part of the story. The viewing habits of the average American family indicate more about television's scope of influence.

Listen to the following statistics: In 1950, the average number of television viewing hours per home was 4.58. The amount of daily viewing time per family steadily increased to 5.93 hours in 1970 and to 6.73 hours in 1980, and reached 6.88 hours in 1994.

The research shows that women watch the most television daily (with 4.42 hours per day), men come in second with 3.75 hours, teens watch an average of 2.77 hours per day, and children under age twelve watch the least, with 2.72 hours daily. (Children between ages 1 and 2 watch about 2 hours a day.) Though children and teens watch less than adults, the amount of daily time devoted to television viewing is astounding. Think about the impact in the lives of children and teens over the span of a year, or a lifetime. Statisticians estimate that in one year the average child watches 1,300 hours of television. By the age of 18, he or she will have watched 20,000 hours.

When you consider the number of family hours per day spent in front of the television, you can begin to understand the influence that television has in the modern American home. Think about any other item of property that most American homes have . . . say, for an example, a bicycle. Think of the difference in lives of the family members if they spent nearly seven hours daily riding a bicycle! (I'm sure the number of dieters across the U.S. would decline!) What if the item were a book . . . how would reading seven hours per day change your life, your goals, your ideas about your world?

Some say that television viewing is a family activity, and it can lead to discussions arising from the issues and events portrayed on the TV. However, since nearly 50 percent of children between ages 6 and 17 have a television set in their bedroom, we can presume that the children are watching alone.

So you can see, television holds a dominant position in our society. From the number of television sets owned to the hours viewed daily, and the nature of that viewing, statistics show us that television is currently a great part of each of our lives.

References

Goleman, Daniel. "Studies Reveal TV's Potential to Teach Infants." *New York Times*, November 22, 1994, p. C1.

Monush, B. *1995 International Television and Video Almanac.* New York: Quigley Publishing Company, Inc., 1995.

Trelease, J. *The Read-Aloud Handbook.* New York: Penguin Books, 1995.

"TV 'Profoundly' Influences Children's Lives, Survey Shows." Cox News Service, September 26, 1991; based upon Yankelovitch Youth Monitor national survey for Corporation for Public Broadcasting.

C./D./E. Answers will vary.

III. What's On?

Techniques

In this short section, students learn about typical genres of television programming and the concept of "prime time." In Activity A, students read descriptions of various television programs and decide which show(s) they would watch and why. In Activity B, the students are asked to match a list of programming genres to the descriptions from Activity A. After reading a short passage on prime-time television in Activity C, the students are asked to orally paraphrase some information from the passage (Activity D). In Activity E, they then return to the television descriptions provided in Activity A and are asked to apply the definition of prime time to the appropriate programs. In the next section, "Television Ratings," the students are given a list of more recent prime-time television programs in the United States.

Answers

A.   Answers will vary.

B.
Gum Drop Safari = Children's program
Yours for the Taking = Game/quiz
Life and Death = Medical drama or soap opera
Audrey = Talk show
Pepperoni = Sitcom
Story of Their Lives = Soap opera or drama

D.   Answers will vary.

E.   *Life and Death, Pepperoni,* and *Story of Their Lives* would be appropriate for prime time as they all have characters and story lines that continue from one show to the next, and they fall into the category of comedy or drama. Generally, talk shows, children's programs, and game shows are not shown during prime-time hours.

IV. Television Ratings

Techniques

The purposes of this section are to familiarize students with how American television shows are rated and to ask them to interpret and calculate the ratings of popular shows. In Activity A and Activity B, students are asked to recognize and correct several subject-verb agreement problems. If you feel students need more work in this area, additional subject-verb exercises are provided here after Activity B. Activity C tests comprehension of the reading and might be done as homework. For Activity D, students are given an authentic example of a television ratings chart and asked to analyze it. You might want to supplement this activity with more recent and/or local ratings of popular television shows.

Answers

A./B.   The number in parentheses indicates the number of the rule that applies to that error.

More than 97 percent of homes in this country *contain* (2) a television, so it isn't easy for the television industry to determine how many people are watching a certain show on any given night. One of the most well-respected television ratings systems in America, however, *is* (3) currently compiled by the A. C. Nielsen Company.

There *are* (4) several methods used by the Nielsen company to compile its data. First, the company *places* (6) small black boxes on the television sets of over 4,000 homes (containing over 10,000 participants) around the country. Each time one of these "wired" sets *is* (3) turned on, the box records the time of day, the channel being watched, and any changes in channels. Every night, the information *is* (6) collected and compiled in a central computer. From the number of actual viewers of a specific program, the company can *estimate* (1) the number of people watching around the country (one Nielsen rating point represents about 954,000 homes, whether or not all those homes are actually tuned in).

Personal information about viewers (such as age, sex, income, and educational level) *is* (2, 6) also collected through the black boxes and, on the local level, through television "diaries," which *are* (5) surveys mailed to as many as 100,000 people, four times a year. Nielsen gathers additional information on the local level through 200 local television markets which *do* (5) their own surveys and polls within specific areas of the country.

In order to ensure accuracy, Nielsen constantly "cross-checks" the information obtained from the different samples and measurements and *conducts* (2) regular quality checks and audits to monitor whether its own procedures are working correctly.

Adapted from *Changing Channels*, Charren Sandler and Martin Sandler, 1981, and personal communication with the A. C. Nielsen Co., Chicago, IL, 1995.

The Nielsen ratings are taken very seriously by the television industry, and especially by advertisers, because they provide estimates about the number of people watching a particular show: who they are, where they live, how much education they *have* (4), and what they like to buy. Nevertheless, the ratings system has been criticized for focusing more on the quantitative (or actual number of viewers) than on the viewers' qualitative feelings and attitudes. The ratings also say nothing about the quality of the programs being watched. Finally, some critics point out that numerical estimates and statistics can be misleading; when one Nielsen home turns on *The Simpsons,* does it really mean that 954,000 other homes are also watching?

C.
1. Nielsen's data indicates how many people are watching a particular show on any given night (television ratings).
2. Cross-checking information from different samples and measurements, regular quality checks, and audits.
3. Advertisers can use this data to target a particular and/or large audience.
4. over 10,000
5. The ratings focus too much on the quantitative (not enough on the qualitative), say nothing about the quality of programs, and may contain misleading numerical estimates and statistics.

D. 1. Thursday   2. Friday   3. Network and Duration
4. $21.1 \times 954,000 = 20,129,400$

Additional Activity

The following examples can be used for further practice with subject-verb agreement.

1. The television series _____ interesting. (look)
2. She always _____ the news on channel 10. (watch)
3. One of the boys _____ upstairs, but the two girls _____ downstairs. (sleep)
4. The woman who she works for _____ her a good salary. (pay)
5. There _____ no cars in the parking lot. (be)
6. Russia _____ a large population. (have)
7. Either the teacher or the students _____ the board. (erase)
8. There _____ no bread left for sandwiches. (be)
9. Her hair _____ clean, but mine _____ dirty. (look)
10. Her dinner _____ not cooked long enough, but mine _____ overcooked. (be)
11. The squirrel _____ nuts, _____ a hole in the ground, and _____ its food for the winter. (collect/dig/store)
12. My sister loves her computer, which _____ on all day. (stay)
13. There _____ a load of furniture in the moving van. (be)
14. Your interests and ideas _____ on your parent's teachings. (depend)
15. The students are the ones who _____ the most power in a classroom. (have)
16. A lot of the bread _____ old and crusty. (seem)
17. No wine _____ better than yours. (taste)
18. Everybody _____ help when they have problems. (need)
19. Anyone who _____ to that music is crazy! (listen)

Answers

1. looks 2. watches 3. sleeps; sleep 4. pays 5. are 6. has
7. erases 8. is 9. looks; looks 10. is; is 11. collects, digs,
stores 12. stays 13. is 14. depend 15. have 16. seems
17. tastes 18. needs 19. listens

V. Dramatization—"A Name for Death"

Techniques

The purposes of this section are to act out and interpret an authentic
television drama and to infer information concerning the characters, plot,
setting, and mood. Activity A serves as a warm-up to the drama. Ask students to try to guess what the scene will be about from the short piece of
provided script. Later, ask students to return to this exercise to see if they
were correct. In Activity B, students read for the main idea of the drama.
Activity D is a review of the drama and of some more difficult idiomatic
expressions. Review these idioms carefully with students, because they will
be asked to produce them in section VI. For Activity E, ask groups to stand
up and act out the scene. By now, students should be comfortable acting in
class. For the questions in Activity F, tell students that some of the answers
are presented in the text and some need to be inferred.

A. Answers will vary. Students should be able to understand that (1) Carol
is Mr. Larabee's secretary and seems to be honest and subservient to
Mr. Larabee, (2) Virginia is his niece and seems to be rather bossy, and
(3) Mr. Larabee is rich, tight with his money, grouchy, tough, independent, and cynical. They may also guess that he is blind because of the
reference to Carol reading the real estate report to him.

C. c

D.
  1. *to have the heart to* = to have the inner strength to
  2. *to carry out orders* = to put into practice
  3. *to make out a check* = to fill in/complete
  4. *to try to get something through someone's head* = to try to make
      someone understand
  5. *to salt away something* = to save something very carefully
  6. *to gyp someone* = to cheat someone
  7. *to wear something or someone a little thin* = demanding too much
      time/energy/patience from someone

8. *to be fed up with something or someone* = to be sick and tired of something or someone
9. *to not stand something or someone* = to be unable to endure something or someone
10. *to (not) give a hang* = to not care at all

F. Possible answers include the following.

1. *Carol Hampton:* tense, nervous; eager to please; secretary to Mr. Larabee; efficient; honest; subservient; and accurate
   Michael F. Larabee: retired, wealthy, blind bachelor; former businessman; used to giving orders; grouchy; careful with money; tough and independent
   Virginia Linton: wife of Mr. Larabee's nephew; bossy; snobbish; energetic
2. Virginia wants to be Mr. Larabee's friend, but she is getting tired of his negative attitude and his insults toward her. She doesn't seem to care much about Carol.
3. Answers will vary.
4. It is too short to be seen in the theater. Also, it would have been more difficult to convey Carol's facial expressions in the last scenes. Michael Larabee's blindness would not have been conveyed well on the radio.

VI. Writing and Acting

Techniques

The purpose of this section is to give students the opportunity to create and act in an original dramatic scene. Remind students that they should use their knowledge of the characters, setting, situation, and so on, from section V to make a believable continuation. For Activity A, remind students that their drama should give some sort of logical explanation/ending to the previous scene. In addition, they should include idiomatic expressions. For Activity B, student groups take turns performing for the rest of the class. If you have access to a video camera, ask students to tape their scenes and to consider camera angles. The scale given in Activity B is not intended to make students nervous or afraid to perform. It is, however, intended to make students more serious about their performance, to ensure that the other students listen carefully to each performance, and to spur discussion of the scenes.

Answers

A./B./C. Answers will vary.

D. *(She picks up the checks Michael has signed and very deliberately tears them up, then puts them in ashtray and burns them. While they are burning, she opens drawer, takes out a new set of checks which she glances over. As she looks, she smiles, then sits down to sign the checks with Michael's signature. Blackout.)*

Chapter 6

Drama in the Movies

Opening Activity

The purpose of this activity is to tap into students' preexisting knowledge of the movies, movie terms, and grammar discussed within this chapter. Students are not expected to be able to answer all the game questions. They should not be frustrated, however, as all the answers will be found in the chapter.

Objective: To finish the game with the largest number of points
Equipment: Game boards, answer key game board, dice

Game Instructions

1. Arrange students into teams (or pairs) and give each team one die.
2. The first team rolls the die, moves ahead the number of spaces shown on the die, and tries to answer the question or follows the instructions to move ahead, move back, or lose a turn.
3. If the team answers the question correctly, they are given one point. The team then rolls again and moves forward to the next question.
4. If the team answers incorrectly, they are given zero points, and they must pass the die to the next team.
5. Play continues until both teams reach the Finish box. The Finish box can be reached either by landing exactly on the space or by overshooting the space, according to the roll of the die.

Game Answer Key

START	C. sitcom	B. sponsor	False	MOVE AHEAD ONE SPACE	C. science fiction	B. stereotype
						A. mediator
B. stereotype	LOSE ONE TURN	True	*Friday the 13th*	C. Westerns	True	A. phrase qualifier
C. a scientist						
Humphrey Bogart	MOVE AHEAD TWO SPACES	True	B. provocative statement	C. gardening	to make up	MOVE AHEAD THREE SPACES
						C. animation
FINISH	A. musical	MOVE BACK FOUR SPACES	False	*Sleepless in Seattle*	MOVE AHEAD THREE SPACES	C. commercial

Objectives for Students

Content

Define and describe common movie genres
Differentiate between generalizations and stereotypes
Identify situations of conflict and resolution strategies
Improvise movie scenes
Analyze, discuss and act a scene from a famous American movie

Language

Reading/Writing

Identifying purpose in writing
Writing introductory paragraphs
Defining and describing
Recognizing and using phrasal qualifiers
Identifying resolution strategies
Inferencing

Speaking/Listening

Brainstorming
Expressing opinions
Explaining facts
Interviewing
Improvising scenes with conflict and resolution
Note-taking
Acting out an authentic movie scene

Chapter Activities

I. Movie Genres

Techniques

In this section students are given more detailed information about some popular movie genres. In Activity A, ask students to read each movie summary and pair it with the genre that comes closest to a match. Tell students that movie genres sometimes overlap and that answers may vary. However, students should be able to defend their answers. Once the students have correctly finished the activity, you may want to ask them if they know the titles of the movies described. Activity B is a quick brainstorm and may bring up additional genres that are not discussed in this chapter. These genres can be used for additional discussion or student reports. Activity D tests reading comprehension while Activity E tests both comprehension and inferencing ability. In Activity F students write an introductory paragraph for the reading. A possible introductory paragraph is included in the teacher's manual and may be shown later for comparison. Activity G gives students a chance to classify their favorite movies, as well as current movies, according to genre. This activity will work with either American or other films.

Answers

A.

1. d horror   *Halloween*
2. h science fiction   *E.T.—The Extra-Terrestrial*
3. g romance   *Casablanca*
4. i Western   *Shane*
5. c. detective   *The Thirty-Nine Steps*
6. e. musical   *Annie*
7. f. political   *Mr. Smith Goes to Washington*
8. b. animation   *Aladdin*
9. a. action/adventure   *Raiders of the Lost Ark*

B. Answers will vary.
Possible answers include the following.

war, epic, documentary, comedy, romantic comedy, fantasy, and so on

C. to define and describe various movie genres

D.

Genre	Central Character	Plot Summary	Example Movies
Action/ adventure	strong hero with a mission	fast-paced; physical or violent series of activities	*Tarzan the Ape Man, Raiders of the Lost Ark, The Terminator, First Blood, Superman*
Animation	lovable talking animals, kings and queens, magic kingdoms	based on comics and fairy tales, contain clear moral messages, happy endings	*Snow White and the Seven Dwarfs, Beauty and the Beast, Aladdin, The Hunchback of Notre Dame*

Genre	Central Character	Plot Summary	Example Movies
Detective	intelligent, cynical, independent individual; secretary or friend	detective is hired to solve crime; often willing to be in danger or break the law; discovers criminal and kills or turns in to the police	*The Maltese Falcon, Chinatown, The Adventures of Sherlock Holmes, The Fugitive*
Horror	the villain, the monster, and the hero	hero must save society from villain's insane, evil intentions or monster	*Frankenstein, King Kong, Friday the 13th, A Nightmare on Elm Street*
Musical	singers and dancers	not complicated or controversial; lighthearted	*Jazz Singer, Singin' in the Rain, Oklahoma!, West Side Story, Annie*
Political	charismatic leader or members of the downtrodden masses	can be realistic; may want viewers to support a political ideology	*Mr. Smith Goes to Washington, The Grapes of Wrath, JFK*

Genre	Central Character	Plot Summary	Example Movies
Romance	two good-hearted people in love with each other	couple is divided and must go through some struggle to come together; ending can be happy (marriage) or sad (death or permanent separation)	Gone with the Wind, Casablanca, Sleepless in Seattle, The Bridges of Madison County
Science fiction	scientist-explorer; beings from either another time or another planet	deals with the idea of space and/or time travel and life in a different place and time	2001: A Space Odyssey, Star Wars, E.T.—The Extra-Terrestrial, Alien
Western	cowboy or sheriff and the villain	villain threatens law and order; hero must protect society	The Searchers, Red River, The Gunfighter, High Noon, Shane

E.
1. Answers will vary.
2. Answers will vary.
3. to make it clear that one political ideology is superior to another
4. family snobbery, the couple's own foolishness, another physical force (i.e., distance)
5. because it deals with the idea of space and time travel and fantastic visions of life in a different place and time
6. The villain is either killed or chased out of town.

F.   Answers will vary.

Possible introductory paragraph

Can you imagine Arnold Schwarzenegger dancing and singing in a musical? Or two space aliens riding on horseback to catch an outlaw? As moviegoers, we expect certain characters and situations to appear in certain types of movies. These types, or genres, of movies can be defined according to the plots, characters, and conflicts they typically contain. Although there may be some overlap in these characteristics, we can generally classify each movie into a particular genre. Some of the most popular genres include action/adventure, animation, detective, horror, musical, political, romantic, science fiction, and the Western.

G.   Answers will vary.

Additional Activity

Using the brainstorming list from Activity B, have students prepare written reports on different popular genres (e.g., war, epic, comedy, documentary, etc.).

II. Hollywood: Fact and Fiction

Techniques

The purpose of this section is to consider how facts and stereotypes are commonly used in movies. In Activity A students decide whether the statements describing American movies are facts or stereotypes. It is important that students give their own opinions without help from the teacher. Activity B is a speaking/listening exercise that asks students to interview Americans. If Americans aren't accessible, this activity will work with other nationalities. This should be done outside of class as homework. Activity C is a discussion of the answers in Activity B. Activity D asks students to think about the definition of a stereotype and is a warm-up for the box on phrasal qualifiers. For Activity E students change stereotypes to generalizations. An alternative activity using phrasal qualifiers is given in the teacher's manual following the answers for Activities E and F. Activity F provides for discussion of students' own cultures.

Answers

A. 1. b (stereotype)   2. b (stereotype)   3. b (stereotype)   4. b (stereotype)   5. a (fact)   6. a (fact)   7. b (stereotype)   8. a (fact)
9. b (stereotype)   10. b (stereotype)

C. Answers will vary

D. This sentence is *not* a stereotype because of the use of the word *most.* It
is a generalization.

E./F. Answers will vary.

Additional Activity

Use qualifiers to write two sentences for each of the following ideas. Your first sentence should be a generalization and your second should point out an exception.

Example: good study habits

As a rule, students need good study habits to succeed. Of course, this does not include Ivan, who seems to succeed without much study.

1. universities
2. foreign languages
3. computers
4. beauty
5. movies
6. your teacher
7. yourself

III. Conflict and Resolution

Techniques

Although there are very few "correct" answers in this section, it may be one of the most challenging in the book. In this section students think about conflicts and resolutions that are prevalent in their own lives. They are then asked to use their preexisting language skills to improvise actual scenes of conflict and resolution. Improvisation can be quite difficult for students, especially if they are used to reading words from a script. Be sure to encourage shyer students and to remind them that there are no incorrect answers. Their greatest challenge in this section is to actually communicate in English for an extended period of time—something that they will have to do each time they have a conversation in English!

Activities A, B, and C are all warm-up activities that tap into students' existing knowledge and language skills. As these activities ask students for personal information, answers will vary. Activity A asks students to think about common causes of conflict in their lives, and then compare their lists with those of other students in Activity B. Activity C asks students to think about how they resolve their problems. Activity D asks students to identify various resolution strategies, and, in Activity E, they are asked to produce the appropriate English for certain resolution strategies. In Activity F, students are asked to identify the conflict in a short dramatic excerpt that prepares them for the later improvisation. This activity should not be skipped, because it is also part of the longer dramatic scene given in section IV. For Activity G students should not be given much time to prepare. Stress to students that improvisations are meant to imitate spontaneous, natural conversation. Remind students that they can use the words and phrases of conflict/resolution found throughout this chapter. Activity H asks students to identify resolutions and also gives students additional practice at improvisations.

Answers

A./B./C. Answers will vary.

D.
  1. bringing up future events
  2. accepting responsibility
  3. avoidance
  4. bringing up past events

5. self-destructive behavior
6. expressing regret
7. discussion
8. physical threat
9. apology
10. finding a mediator

E.

Apologizing
I'm very sorry.
Forgive me, I'm terribly sorry about . . .
I apologize.

Accepting responsibility
I don't know why I did this. It was foolish of me.
This is completely my fault.
I know I am responsible.

Discussion
I understand why you're upset, but I think we need to talk more about
  the problem.
Is this something we can discuss?
Don't be angry. Let's talk it over.
Why don't we talk about it over lunch?

Finding a mediator
Let's see what (mediator) thinks.
I'd really like to hear an objective opinion.
Why don't we ask an expert?
Don't you think we should ask someone else?

Offering a solution
I think the best solution is . . .
Instead of arguing, why don't we just . . .
I've got an idea! We should . . .
It really would be better if . . .

F. Ilsa wants something from Richard, but Richard does not seem to trust
     her.

G./H./I. Answers will vary.

IV. Dramatization—*Casablanca*

Techniques

In this section the students learn more about the movie *Casablanca* and are asked to improvise and perform scenes from it. In Activity A, students listen to a brief synopsis of the movie and take notes. Based on their notes, students improvise a scene in Activity B. In Activity C, students read an actual scene from *Casablanca.* They can read the scene silently or aloud in pairs. Resolution strategies are recycled in Activity D, and Activity E tests students' comprehension and inferencing ability based on the information in the scene. For Activity F, allow pairs sufficient time to prepare a dramatization of the scene. Because this is the last dramatization in the book, a grading scale has been included in the student book. Make sure that students know that this drama presentation will be "graded."

Answers

A.

Script

The setting of the movie *Casablanca* is the island of Casablanca. The movie takes place during the politically unstable early years of World War II. Much of the action takes place in a popular, chic nightclub called "Rick's Café." In the opening scenes we are introduced to three main characters, Rick Blain, Ilsa Lund, and Victor Laszlo.

First we meet the young, single owner of Rick's Café, Richard (Rick) Blain. Rick is a wealthy, well-connected, and powerful man in Casablanca. In the past, he was a politically passionate man and was willing to sacrifice his life for his beliefs. Now, however, Rick is a cynical and detached businessman, and he continually repeats the sentence, "I stick my neck out for nobody." Second, we meet the sophisticated and startlingly beautiful Ilsa Lund. Ilsa, who has been working in the French underground movement against the Nazis, is desperately trying to escape the Nazis and travel through Casablanca to America with her husband (the third main character), Victor Laszlo. Victor is a brave and courageous man. He has completely devoted himself to working in the French underground movement and is not afraid to sacrifice his life for his strong beliefs. The Nazis know that Victor has been working against them, and they know he is in Casablanca. If they catch him, it will lead to his arrest and, perhaps, his death.

In brief, the plot summary of *Casablanca* is this: In the past, Ilsa and Rick met in Paris, fell deeply in love, and made plans to run away together. During this time, Ilsa thought that her husband (Victor Laszlo) was dead. After discovering that Victor was still alive, however, Ilsa left Rick and broke his heart. Now, however (in Casablanca), Ilsa and Victor both need Rick's help.

Because he is a well-connected and powerful man in Casablanca, Rick possesses two official "Letters of Transit." Ilsa and Victor desperately need these letters so that they might travel freely to North or South America. Without the letters, they will both certainly be caught by the Nazis.

D.
1. demanding a solution
2. dismissing the problem
3. bringing up past events
4. insult
5. apology
6. physical threat/demanding a solution
7. explanation
8. claiming ignorance
9. avoidance
10. expressing regret

E.
1. No. Rick says, "I'm not fighting for anything anymore, except myself. I'm the only cause I'm interested in."
2. Ilsa admires Laszlo and wants to save his life. She is still in love with Rick.
3. Ilsa was afraid that if she told Rick the truth he would not leave Paris and would be caught by the Gestapo.
4. Answers will vary.
5. In the end, Rick gives the Letters of Transit to Ilsa. Ilsa had planned to give the Letters of Transit to Victor and to stay behind with Rick. However, at the airport, Rick tells Ilsa to go with Victor, because she belongs with Victor and he can't do his work without her. Ilsa does not want to go, but she knows deep in her heart it is the right decision.

Additional Activity

Have the students improvise an ending to the movie or a continuation of the scene provided.

F. Grade each scene according to the following scale.

1.	Were the setting and location of the scene clearly indicated?	10%
2.	Were the movements and gestures appropriate?	15%
3.	Were appropriate props and/or pictures used?	10%
4.	Did every actor remain "in character"?	25%
5.	Were any actions of the original scene omitted?	15%
6.	Was any dialogue of the original scene omitted?	10%
7.	Was the length of the scene appropriate?	15%
	Possible Total	100%
	Actual Total	_____